Little Pebble™

T0077081

# Community Helpers at the Construction Site

by Mari Schuh

CAPSTONE PRESS
a capstone imprint

Little Pebble is published by Capstone Press,
1710 Roe Crest Drive, North Mankato, Minnesota 56003
www.mycapstone.com

Copyright © 2017 by Capstone Press, a Capstone imprint. All rights reserved. No part of this publication may be reproduced in whole or in part, or stored in a retrieval system, or transmitted in any form or by any means, electronic, mechanical, photocopying, recording, or otherwise, without written permission of the publisher.

**Library of Congress Cataloging-in-Publication Data**
Names: Schuh, Mari C., 1975– author.
Title: Community helpers at the construction site / by Mari Schuh.
Description: North Mankato, Minnesota : Little Pebble Books, an imprint of Capstone Press, [2017] | Series: Little pebble. Community helpers on the scene | Audience: Ages 4–8. | Audience: K to grade 3. | Includes bibliographical references and index. Identifiers: LCCN 2016009760|
ISBN 9781515724018 (library binding) | ISBN 9781515724117 (pbk.) |
ISBN 9781515724186 (ebook (pdf)) | ISBN 9798875202841 (pbk)
Subjects: LCSH: Construction workers—Juvenile literature. |
Construction industry—Juvenile literature. Classification: LCC TH159 .S38 2017 |
DDC 690—dc23
LC record available at http://lccn.loc.gov/2016009760

**Editorial Credits**
Megan Atwood, editor; Juliette Peters, designer;
Pam Mitsakos, media researcher; Tori Abraham, production specialist

**Photo Credits**
Alamy Images: Nik Taylor, 17; Getty Images: Huntstock_Images, 12-13, Yellow Dog Productions, 4-5; iStockphoto: IPGGutenbergUKLtd, 11; Shutterstock: Andrey_Popov, 18-19, bikeriderlondon, cover, Dmitry Kalinovsky, 14-15, kasahasa, 3, 24, back cover, kurhan, 20-21, Maria Jeffs, 8-9, michaeljung, 6-7, mihalec, 1

Printed and bound in the USA. 5884

# Table of Contents

A New Home . . . . . 4

At the Job Site . . . . . 6

Glossary . . . . . 22
Read More . . . . . 23
Index . . . . . 24

# A New Home

Workers come to a job site.

They will build a home.

Who helps at the site?

# At the Job Site

Here is the foreman.

He leads the crew.

Let's go!

A machine operator digs.

He moves the dirt.

CASE
EXTENDAHOE
AMULET
CASE

A framer makes a wall.

It is tall.

Up it goes!

Look up!

A roofer makes a roof.

It is big.

He uses nails.

A mason lays bricks.

He will add stones too.

Good job!

An electrician puts in wires.

She uses pliers.

A plumber adds pipes.

He uses a wrench.

Many helpers work
at a job site.
They get the job done.

30'
30'
30'

# Glossary

**electrician**—a worker who puts in and fixes electrical items

**foreman**—the leader of a group of workers

**framer**—a worker who nails wood together to make a building's walls

**machine operator**—a worker who drives a machine

**mason**—a worker who builds or works with bricks, stones, or cement

**plumber**—a worker who puts in pipes or repairs pipes

**roofer**—a worker who builds the roof of a building by adding tiles or shingles

# Read More

**Deedrick, Tami.** *Construction Workers Help.* Our Community Helpers. North Mankato, Minn.: Capstone Press, 2014.

**Heos, Bridget.** *Let's Meet a Construction Worker.* Community Helpers. Minneapolis: Millbrook Press, 2013.

**Jeffries, Joyce.** *Meet the Construction Worker.* People Around Town. New York: Gareth Stevens Publishing, 2014.

# Index

electricians, 16
foremen, 6
framers, 10
helpers, 20
homes, 4
machine operators, 8
masons, 14
pliers, 16
plumbers, 18
roofers, 12
workers, 4
wrenches, 18